THE LOONEY TUNES SONGBOOK

Alfred

Produced by
Alfred Music Publishing Co., Inc.
P.O. Box 10003
Van Nuys, CA 91410-0003
alfred.com

D0916173

Printed in USA.

ISBN-10: 0-7390-7120-3
ISBN-13: 978-0-7390-7120-5

Thanks to Leith Adams, Jerry Beck, Joseph Billé, Jeff Briggs, Irwin Chusid, Ned Comstock, Les Deutsch, Rick Gehr, Brian Gari, Daniel Goldmark, Sandra Joy Lee, Lisa Margolis, Alex Rannie, and the USC Warner Bros. archives.

 Alfred Cares. Contents printed on 100% recycled paper.
Except pages 1–4 which are printed on 60% recycled paper.

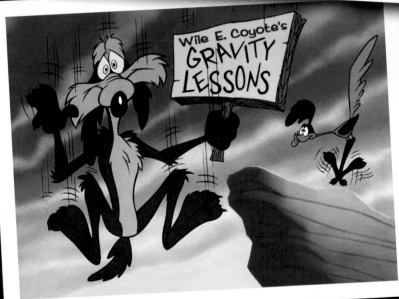

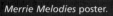

Merrie Melodies poster.

Michigan J. Frog sings
"Hello! Ma Baby"
in *One Froggy Evening*.

Bugs Bunny sings
"A Rainy Night in Rio"
in *Long-Haired Hare*.

"Owl Jolson" in
I Love to Singa.

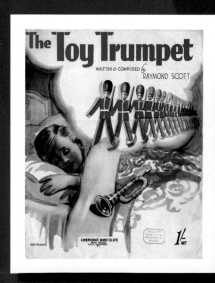

Contents

Cartoon Music

Countless members of the baby boomer generation received their musical indoctrination not from radio or phonograph records, but from the soundtracks to animated cartoons viewed in theaters and on Saturday morning television. During these six- to eight-minute shorts, impressionable youngsters were exposed to a dizzying array of musical styles that were seared into their collective unconscious. Classical music, opera, folk songs, pop ditties, jazz, swing, world music, and even early rock 'n' roll all received equal time in the scores that accompanied animated featurettes. One of the most prolific companies to dispense this passive musical education was Warner Bros., whose *Merrie Melodies* and *Looney Tunes* cartoons feature a relentless onslaught of musical references. Although initially viewed as a subject not worthy of serious study, cartoon music is now considered an art form in itself, and today is the subject of in-depth analysis in essays, books, and university studies.

This songbook celebrates the music produced for Warner Bros. for the *Merrie Melodies* and *Looney Tunes* cartoons. During most of this period, the studio's musical mastermind was Carl Stalling, a visionary whose genius for linking music to the frenetic action on the screen became the gold standard for animation scoring.

Carl Stalling, the genius behind the Warner Bros. cartoon scores.

Stalling got his start working for Walt Disney. He was eventually hired by Warner Bros., and until his retirement 22 years later, he produced hundreds of scores for cartoons starring the icons of the *Looney Tunes* empire, including Bugs Bunny, Daffy Duck, Elmer Fudd, Porky Pig, the Road Runner, and many more.

Although Stalling used hundreds of titles to provide musical accents for Warner Bros. cartoons, a select group of songs stand out, either by association with cartoons that are considered classics today or because they were used on multiple occasions. This songbook, although by no means definitive, includes what we consider to be some of the most memorable musical moments from those cartoons.

Merrie Melodies and *Looney Tunes* Themes

The series names *Merrie Melodies* and *Looney Tunes* were inspired by Disney's *Silly Symphonies*. Their themes were pop songs published by Warner Bros., used as title sequence underscoring. The jaunty theme for the *Merrie Melodies* series, "Merrily We Roll Along," was written by Charlie Tobias, Murray Mencher, and Eddie Cantor. The *Looney Tunes* theme, "The Merry-Go-Round Broke Down," was written by Dave Franklin and Cliff Friend. To this song, we have added an alternate refrain, as sung by Daffy Duck in *Daffy Duck and Egghead*. Carl Stalling wrote a third theme, "What's Up, Doc?" which became associated with the studio's leading character, Bugs Bunny.

Many of the Warner Bros. cartoons were showcased in a new television series, *The Bugs Bunny/Road Runner Hour*, which was initially broadcast on ABC. The series featured new sequences that created continuity with existing cartoons. A new theme song titled "This Is It!" was written by Jerry Livingston and Mack David to start each episode, with Bugs Bunny and Daffy Duck serving as the show's dual hosts.

The battling desert characters, the Road Runner and Wile E. Coyote, headlined another half-hour series. For that series, the theme song "Road Runner" was introduced, which was written and performed by Barbara Cameron.

Raymond Scott Songs

In assembling his scores, Carl Stalling relied on a musical arsenal consisting of a variety of styles. While working for Disney, he was restricted to using material in the public domain (classical and folk music from the 19th century and earlier), but at Warner Bros., Stalling was able to use anything from the vast Warner Bros. publishing holdings. As a result, he sprinkled his soundtrack with quotations from many popular songs from Warner films, which were used not only as background music, but were on many occasions sung by characters on screen. In addition, Stalling made frequent use of music written by composer Raymond Scott, whose quirky, offbeat three-minute miniatures were written for his jazz combo, the Raymond Scott Quintette.

Producer Chuck Jones at work. Standing are possibly Lloyd Vaughn (left) and Ken Harris (right) of Warner Bros.

Ideally suited for cartoons, Scott's songs are characterized by breakneck-pace tempos, twitchy rhythms, and melodies that behave like a shorting circuit. (It amazes *Looney Tunes* fans when they discover that not only did Scott never write music with cartoons in mind, he didn't even like watching cartoons.) With their appropriately idiosyncratic titles, Scott's compositions turned up in over 100 Warner Bros. cartoons. Their staying power remains relevant today, as some of Scott's songs continue to make appearances on soundtracks for more recent animated series like *The Ren and Stimpy Show*, *The Simpsons*, *Animaniacs*, and a myriad of programs featured on cable television's Cartoon Network.

The most pervasive and familiar of Scott's songs is "Powerhouse," which consists of two distinctive melodies. The first is a rapidly rising series of half-step figures that gives the impression of a frantic chase sequence. The second melody is characterized by a bass line that brings to mind an automated assembly line gone amok. "Powerhouse" was used mainly in sequences featuring conveyor belts or other kinds of machinery. In addition to being included in over 40 Warner cartoons, it was also used in the film *Looney Tunes: Back in Action*, the 2003 tribute to the golden age of Warner Bros. cartoons.

"Dinner Music for a Pack of Hungry Cannibals" was used in many toons as well, but most notably in underscoring the title sequence to *Gorilla My Dreams*, which starred Bugs Bunny as a castaway who lands on a jungle island only to be selected for adoption by the childless Mrs. Gruesome Gorilla.

Scott adapted the melody for "In an Eighteenth Century Drawing Room" from Mozart's Piano Sonata No. 16 in C Major, but added jazzy variations on the theme that took it into the 20th century. Among the cartoons in which it is featured are *Bugs Bunny and the Three Bears* and *A Streetcat Named Sylvester*.

"The Toy Trumpet" is one of Scott's sprightlier melodies, featured in *Daffy—The Commando* and *Rebel Rabbit*. With lyrics written by Sidney D. Mitchell and Lew Pollack, it was sung by Shirley Temple in the 1938 film *Rebecca of Sunnybrook Farm*.

"Reckless Night on Board an Ocean Liner" can be heard in *Hare Lift*, which features an epic battle between Bugs Bunny and Yosemite Sam, and *Jumpin' Jupiter*, featuring Porky Pig and Sylvester in outer space.

Warner Bros. Pop Songs

The initial intent of the Warner Bros. animated cartoons was to exploit the songs in the Warner Bros. publishing catalog. When a cartoon was produced, management often required that a Warner Bros. song was used in the soundtrack. Two former Disney animators inaugurated the *Looney Tunes* series, which was followed by *Merrie Melodies*. The animators' names—Hugh Harman and Rudolf Ising—turned out to be a perfect (albeit accidental) combination; their credit, "Harman-Ising," is a musical pun.

When Carl Stalling joined Warner Bros., he began utilizing the vast resources of the studio's publishing archive to provide a musical reflection of the action. Although he used hundreds of cues throughout his 22-year tenure, Stalling had a selection of favorites, which he would use whenever a particular thematic situation arose. One of the most curious of these was "A Cup of Coffee, a Sandwich, and You," an obscure number written by the team of Billy Rose, Al Dubin, and Joseph Mayer, which underscored any scene featuring food or characters eating.

Bugs Bunny often foiled his antagonists by masquerading in female clothing, and whenever his outfit was red (as in his Red Riding Hood garb in *Now Hare This*), you could count on hearing Mort Dixon and Allie Wrubel's "The Lady in Red," from the Warner Bros. film musical *In Caliente*.

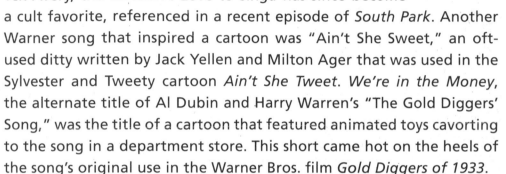

Some Warner songs actually doubled as the titles of cartoons. "I Love to Sing-a" was an early collaboration between E.Y. Harburg and Harold Arlen that was used in a *Merrie Melodies* parody of *The Jazz Singer*, with the song sung by a diminutive bird named Owl Jolson. Directed by Tex Avery, the cartoon *I Love to Singa* has since become a cult favorite, referenced in a recent episode of *South Park*. Another Warner song that inspired a cartoon was "Ain't She Sweet," an oft-used ditty written by Jack Yellen and Milton Ager that was used in the Sylvester and Tweety cartoon *Ain't She Tweet*. *We're in the Money*, the alternate title of Al Dubin and Harry Warren's "The Gold Diggers' Song," was the title of a cartoon that featured animated toys cavorting to the song in a department store. This short came hot on the heels of the song's original use in the Warner Bros. film *Gold Diggers of 1933*.

Many other familiar songs pop up from time to time in Warner cartoons. "I'm Forever Blowing Bubbles" was used in *Catch as Cats Can*, played after Sylvester unwittingly eats a bar of soap. "Hooray for Hollywood," written by Johnny Mercer and Richard A. Whiting, was used in *Daffy Duck in Hollywood* or whenever a character becomes starstruck or somehow ends up in Tinseltown. Another Mercer lyric, "You Must Have Been a Beautiful Baby," with a melody by Harry Warren, was featured in *The Hardship of Miles Standish*, sung by Arthur Q. Bryan as Elmer Fudd.

Animator Tex Avery (left) and producer Fred Quimby (right) at MGM.

The concept of a character actually singing a Warner Bros. song was used frequently. One of the most memorable of these occurs in *Long Haired Hare*, in which Bugs Bunny accompanies himself on the banjo as he sings "A Rainy Night in Rio," an obscure tune from the film musical *The Time, The Place, and the Girl*. The catchy song is annoying enough to disrupt the practicing of opera impresario Giovanni Jones, who absent-mindedly finds himself singing along. This sets off an outrageous series of one-upmanship gags that end with the sonic destruction of the Hollywood Bowl.

One Froggy Evening

One of the most famous uses of music in a Warner Bros. cartoon is *One Froggy Evening*, an outrageously funny and celebrated short that features no dialog, only songs from the early years of the 20th century. In the story, a frog that is buried in a box in a cornerstone of a demolished building emerges to sing vaudeville songs, complete with top hat and cane, but will sing only to the opportunistic construction worker who finds him. For this cartoon, Stalling came up with a series of well-known vintage songs for the frog to perform, including Eubie Blake and Noble Sissle's "I'm Just Wild About Harry" (1921), and Ida Emerson and Joseph E. Howard's "Hello! Ma Baby" (1899). When the script called for a brief snippet from a ragtime song, director Chuck Jones could not come up with anything appropriate, so he and writer Michael Maltese penned a peppy number that they called "The Michigan Rag." The frog and the song became so identified with each other that Jones eventually named the character Michigan J. Frog. "The Michigan Rag" is printed for the very first time in this songbook.

Michael Maltese (left) and Chuck Jones (right) go over a storyboard at the Warner Bros. studios.

The songs in this book are only a sampling of the countless melodies used by Carl Stalling in his *Looney Tunes* and *Merrie Melodies* series. The next time your children (or you) are watching one of the Warner Bros. animated cartoons, turn off the picture and just listen to the soundtrack. You might be amazed at how many wonderful old songs you recognize and want to learn to play or sing for yourself. That's all, folks!

Cary Ginell

Popular Music Editor

Alfred Music Publishing, Inc.

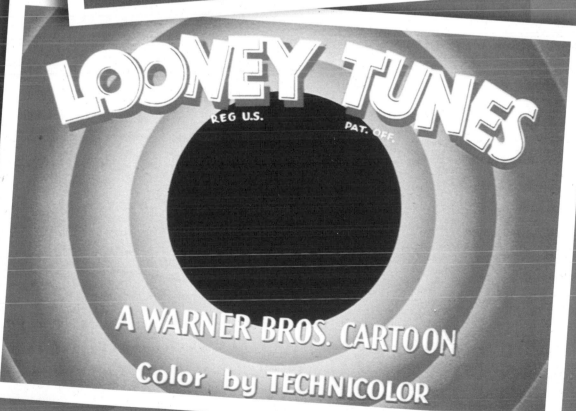

"Merrily We Roll Along" (score)

First pages of the original score for the *Merrie Melodies* theme song, "Merrily We Roll Along." The familiar opening glissando was played on an electric guitar.

MERRILY WE ROLL ALONG

Words and Music by
EDDIE CANTOR, CHARLIE TOBIAS
and MURRAY MENCHER

Too man-y frowns can change the bright-est dis-po-si-tion

as sure as clouds can dark-en the dawn.

Merrily We Roll Along - 4 - 1

ROAD RUNNER

Words and Music by
BARBARA CAMERON

Road Runner, Road Run-ner runs down the road all day.
Poor lit-tle Road Run-ner nev-er both-ers an-y - one. Just

E - ven the Coy - o-te can't make him change his ways.
run-nin' down the road is his i - de-a of hav-in' fun.

Chorus:

Road Run - ner, the Coy - o - te's af - ter

you. Road Run - ner, if he

THE MERRY-GO-ROUND BROKE DOWN

Words and Music by
CLIFF FRIEND and DAVE FRANKLIN

Verse:

Ask me why I'm hap-py sing-ing like a lark,___ and I'll tell you of an old a-muse-ment park.___ A "mer-ry-go-round" was there, I glad-ly paid the fare. My

THIS IS IT!

Words and Music by
MACK DAVID and JERRY LIVINGSTON

This Is It! - 3 - 1

WHAT'S UP, DOC?

Words and Music by
CARL STALLING

Raymond Scott Songs

The Raymond Scott Quintette. Scott is in the foreground, in the control booth. The Quintette features, from left to right: Dave Harris, tenor saxophone; Pete Pumiglio, clarinet; Louis Shoobe, bass; Dave Wade, trumpet; and Johnny Williams, drums. (photo courtesy Irwin Chusid.)

IN AN EIGHTEENTH CENTURY DRAWING ROOM

(Instrumental Version)

Music by
RAYMOND SCOTT

In an Eighteenth Century Drawing Room - 5 - 1

In an Eighteenth Century Drawing Room - 5 - 3

DINNER MUSIC FOR A PACK OF HUNGRY CANNIBALS

Music by
RAYMOND SCOTT

Dinner Music for a Pack of Hungry Cannibals - 4 - 1

POWERHOUSE

Music by
RAYMOND SCOTT

Powerhouse - 6 - 1

Moderately

RECKLESS NIGHT ON BOARD AN OCEAN LINER

Music by
RAYMOND SCOTT

Reckless Night on Board an Ocean Liner - 4 - 1

Reckless Night on Board an Ocean Liner - 4 - 2

Reckless Night on Board an Ocean Liner - 4 - 4

THE TOY TRUMPET
(Instrumental Version)

Music by
RAYMOND SCOTT

The Toy Trumpet - 5 - 1

The Toy Trumpet - 5 - 4

Title cards and art from *Merrie Melodies* and *Looney Tunes* animated shorts that utilize Warner Bros.-published songs.

AIN'T SHE SWEET

Words by
JACK YELLEN

Music by
MILTON AGER

Medium bright

C/E G7/D Am/C E7/B Am7 D13 Dm7/G G7(♭9 ♯5)

(%) Verse:

C C♯dim7 G7 C Cdim7 C G9(♯5) C F6 C

1. There she is!___ There she is!___ There's what keeps me up at night._
2. Tell me where,___ tell me where_ have you seen one just like that?_

Am E7 Am F7 Am Dm6 Am Dm6 Am

Oh, gee whiz!___ Oh, gee whiz!___ There's why I can't eat a bite._
I de - clare,___ I de - clare, that sure is worth look - ing at.___

G7 C6 C9/B♭ A7

Those flam - ing eyes! That flam - ing youth!
Oh boy, how sweet those lips must be!

Ain't She Sweet - 3 - 1

Chorus:

A CUP OF COFFEE,
A SANDWICH, AND YOU

Words by
BILLY ROSE and AL DUBIN

Music by
JOSEPH MEYER

A Cup of Coffee, a Sandwich, and You - 4 - 1

A Cup of Coffee, a Sandwich, and You - 4 - 4

THE GOLD DIGGERS' SONG
(WE'RE IN THE MONEY)

Words by
AL DUBIN

Music by
HARRY WARREN

Gone are my blues, and gone are my tears;

I've got good news to shout in your ears.

The Gold Diggers' Song (We're in the Money) - 4 - 1

The sil-ver dol-lar has re-turned to the fold,_____ with

sil-ver you can turn your dreams to gold._____

We're in the mon-ey, we're in the mon-ey;

we've got a lot of what it takes to get a-long!

The Gold Diggers' Song (We're in the Money) - 4 - 2

HOORAY FOR HOLLYWOOD

Words by
JOHNNY MERCER

Music by
RICHARD A. WHITING

I LOVE TO SING-A

Words by
E.Y. HARBURG

Music by
HAROLD ARLEN

I Love to Sing-A - 6 - 1

I'M FOREVER BLOWING BUBBLES

Words and Music by JOHN KELLETTE,
JAMES BROCKMAN, NAT VINCENT and JAMES KENDIS

Valse lente

1. I'm dream - ing dreams,
2. When sha - dows creep,

I'm schem - ing schemes, I'm build - ing cas - tles high,_____
when I'm a - sleep, to lands of hope I stray,_____

____ they're born a - new, their days are few, just like a
____ then at day - break, when I a - wake, my blue - bird

I'm Forever Blowing Bubbles - 3 - 1

sweet but-ter - fly.___ And as the day-light is
flut - ters a - way.___ Hap - pi - ness, you seem so

dawn ing, they come a - gain in the morn - ing.
near me, hap - pi - ness, come forth and cheer me.

I'm for-ev - er blow - ing bub - bles,___ pret - ty bub-bles

in the air,___ they fly so high, near-ly reach the

I'm Forever Blowing Bubbles - 3 - 2

A RAINY NIGHT IN RIO

Words by
LEO ROBIN

Music by
ARTHUR SCHWARTZ

THE LADY IN RED
(Querida Mujer)

Words by
MORT DIXON

Music by
ALLIE WRUBEL

Moderately

The Lady in Red - 8 - 1

YOU MUST HAVE BEEN A BEAUTIFUL BABY

Lyrics by
JOHNNY MERCER

Music by
HARRY WARREN

Michigan J. Frog in One Froggy Evening.

HELLO! MA BABY

Words and Music by
JOE E. HOWARD and IDA EMERSON

I'M JUST WILD ABOUT HARRY

Words by
NOBLE SISSLE

Music by
EUBIE BLAKE

I'm Just Wild About Harry - 4 - 1

THE MICHIGAN RAG

By MICHAEL MALTESE

The Michigan Rag - 2 - 1

"That's all Folks!"